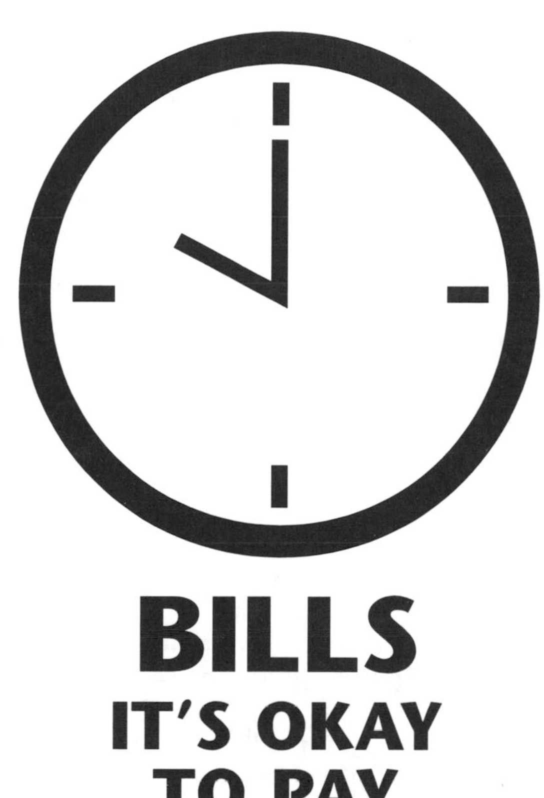

BILLS
IT'S OKAY TO PAY
LATE

Printed in the United States of America

CONTENTS

1 SAVINGS SAVVY

2 THE INVESTMENT GAME

3 MONEY MANAGEMENT

4 TAXPAYER VICTORIES

5 SURVIVING AN AUDIT

1
SAVINGS SAVVY

LITTLE WAYS TO SAVE BIG DOLLARS

Source: **Lee Simmons,** coauthor with his wife, Barbara, of *Penny Pinching: How to Lower Your Everyday Expenses Without Lowering Your Standard of Living.* Bantam Books.

You can slash your expenses without ripping your lifestyle to shreds. We did. The key is to change both your shopping and consuming styles to get the same items at far better prices. Among our favorite ways to save money on everyday purchases...

AT THE GROCERY STORE...

• ***Supermarkets.*** When you shop, always go *alone*—a child or spouse will increase your bill by requesting items you didn't intend to buy. Before you go to the store, make a complete list of what you need. *Reason:* This reduces your own impulse buying.

STRATEGY: Bend and stretch. Best-selling items are usually prominently displayed at eye level. Better deals are usually on the top and bottom shelves.

• ***Use your freezer strategically.*** When meat or poultry is on sale, buy a lot and freeze it.

• ***Shop seasonally.*** When certain seasonal items—such as fruit—are at special, low prices, buy in bulk and freeze.

EXAMPLE: In the East, a pint of strawberries can cost $4 in December and 89 cents in June. (The cheaper pint always tastes better to us.) *Note:* Berries freeze particularly well. You can also "store" fruit by making jams and jellies and by baking—and then freezing—pies.

• ***Avoid convenience rip-offs.*** A 16-ounce package of chopped cabbage and a few carrot bits is labeled "fresh coleslaw" and can cost $1.59. But whole cabbages sell for 49 cents a pound. *Estimated time to chop one pound of cabbage:* Ninety seconds. *Hourly rate being charged for this convenience:* $44.

Salad bars are another high-priced convenience. Instead of getting a fruit salad for lunch—at a cost of $3.99 a pound—buy three different fruits at the grocery store. You'll save $2 or $3—a savings that can amount to hundreds of dollars a year. A salad-bar vegetable salad is also unbelievably expensive compared with what you can make at home.

AROUND THE HOUSE...

• ***Hot water.*** Hot water is usually your second-biggest energy expense. You can save 20% a year by taking these steps...

• Install a programmable water heater control (about $100). How often do you need hot water at 3 am?

• Buy an insulation blanket ($25) to cover your water heater. *Reason:* Water heaters lose heat through the tank walls. This could shave 10% off your annual bill.

• Lower water temperature from 140 degrees to 125 degrees. This lower temperature is fine for showering. *Note:* Some dishwashers require the higher temperature—*so check first.*

• Use a cold-water detergent and cold water for most laundry loads. Only very dirty or greasy laundry needs hot water.

• ***Caulking and weather-stripping.*** *Test:* See if windows and doors need weather-stripping and/or caulking by moving a lighted candle around the frames. You will know if air is passing through.

Caulking and weather-stripping two doors and a dozen windows should cost less than $50. *Result:* You will save 10%, or more, on your annual energy bill, a great return on investment.

• ***Ceiling fans.*** These fans are a great energy saver in both hot and cold months.The fans use less than one-tenth the amount of electricity a standard air conditioner does.

SUMMER STRATEGY: If it's too hot to live with just the ceiling fan, turn on the air conditioner. But—remember, the fan makes the room seem five to seven degrees colder, so adjust the thermostat of your air conditioner accordingly.

WINTER STRATEGY: Turn the fan on after reversing the direction of the blades (buy fans with reversible motors). Because warm air tends to rise toward the ceiling, the fan will help keep warm air where you want it—lower in the room. (The higher the ceiling, the more significant the savings.)

• ***Telephone wire maintenance.*** About 20% of the population pays $2 to $3 a month for telephone wire maintenance. This is unnecessary. The charge is like insurance—it covers you if a telephone company repair person has to fix a wire inside your home. But this rarely happens.

STRATEGY: Call the phone company and get rid of the charge. You'll save $30 a year. Even if you did need in-home phone wire repairs every five years (which is almost unheard of), you'll still come out ahead.

• ***Negotiate.*** Many people don't realize that in many stores, a price tag is merely an asking price, just as it is in a car showroom.

STRATEGY: On big-ticket items, always try to negotiate a better deal. If this doesn't work, offer to pay in cash—it may get you a better price.

KEY: Timing. Shop late in the month, when managers will be most eager to move merchandise (often to meet a monthly quota). This strategy doesn't just work with car dealers. It's successful at electronics stores, clothing retailers, etc.

• ***Buy off-season.*** Air conditioners are cheapest in September, when stores want to unload excess inventory, and in January and February, when sales of all major appliances typically occur. You can get much better buys on lawn furniture and grills in August and September than in May and June. And—those are also good months to buy outdoor cooking utensils, humidifiers and portable heaters.

• ***Buy from mail-order discounters.*** This practice is both convenient and cheap.

FOR TRAVEL...

• ***Travel off-season.*** Around the beginning of June, Caribbean resorts drop prices by as much as 50%...in May, airlines slash rates...and ski resorts give you great off-season values as well. Of course, there won't be snow, but the tennis, golf, hiking and biking can more than make up for that.

• ***Buy airline tickets from a consolidator.*** When airlines can't sell all their seats, they often sell them to a ticket broker—or consolidator—at wholesale prices. Discounts range from 15% to 50%.

NOTE: Consolidators sell directly to travel agents as well as to the general public. Ask your travel agent if any such tickets are available.

WARNING: These tickets are usually nonrefundable, and you may not fly at the most convenient time or take the most direct route. Make sure you're buying a discounted ticket rather than a seat on a charter flight.

• ***Get great hotel deals.*** Deluxe and first-class hotels in major cities offer terrific weekend specials when business traffic is slow. Call the 800 number for Hilton, Hyatt, Ritz-Carlton, Westin, etc., for the city you're interested in. Then call the individual hotel's front desk directly. The rate you are quoted will often be lower than the rate you are given when you call the 800 number.

■

FROM THE COUNTRY'S VERY BEST PENNY-PINCHERS, THE BEST MONEY-SAVING STRATEGIES

SENIOR SPECIALS...

• ***Always ask for discounts.*** Most senior specials are unadvertised. You often don't have to be retirement age to take advantage of them. Start asking for specials the day you turn 50. Ask at banks, hair salons, bus lines—anywhere you're going to be spending money.

From: **Amy Dacyczyn,** author of *The Tightwad Gazette.*

GREAT DIRECT MAIL BUYS...

• ***Bed and bath.*** Save up to 50% on leading brands at Harris Levy, Inc., 278 Grand St., New York 10002. 212-226-3102. Catalog available.

• ***Camera equipment.*** Save up to 35% on cameras and equipment at Porter's Camera Stores, Box 628, Cedar Falls, IA 50613. 800-553-2001. Free catalog.

From: **Sue Goldstein,** author of *Great Buys by Mail (And Phone!).*

• ***Cosmetics and perfume.*** Save up to 75% on Oscar de la Renta, Giorgio, Estée Lauder and others. Beauty Boutique, Box 94520, 6836 Engle Rd., Cleveland 44101. 440-826-1712. Free catalog.

• ***Electronics.*** Save up to 50% at J&R Music World, Customer Service, 15 Park Row, 16th fl., New York 10038. 800-221-8180. http://www. jandr.com. Free catalog.

From: **Prudence McCullough,** executive editor of *Buy Wholesale-by-Mail 1998.*

• ***Golf and tennis gear.*** Buy brand-name equipment through Las Vegas Golf & Tennis, 4211 Paradise Rd., Las Vegas 89109. Call 800-933-7777 for price quotes.

From: **Eric W. Gershman,** author of *400 Steals Beyond Belief.*

TRAVEL AND SAVE...

• ***Use the Internet.*** Major airlines are now selling unsold tickets at deep discounts over the Internet—many of these bargains are not available elsewhere. **EXAMPLES...**

• TWA sells coach tickets at up to 75% off. Available tickets are posted Tuesdays at http://www.twa.com.

• American Airlines lets customers sign up for free E-mail service announcing discounts. E-mail messages are sent out Wednesdays about discounts for the following weekend. Join at http://www.amrcorp.com.

• Continental's program is similar to American's. Sign up at http://www.flycontinental.com.

• US Airways offers savings at http://www.usairways.com.

From: **John Edwards,** a computer industry analyst and writer on high-tech subjects, based in Mount Laurel, NJ.

• ***Split-ticketing.*** Beat the mandatory Saturday-night stay on excursion fares by buying two round-trip discount tickets. **STRATEGY...**

• Ticket A from your hometown to your destination and back.

• Ticket B from your destination to your home and back to your destination.

Use the outbound part of ticket A when you take the trip. Then return using the outbound part of ticket B. The airline won't realize that you didn't stay over on a Saturday. And you have two tickets for your next trip.

CAUTION: Be sure to confirm all legs of all flights—otherwise, the airline may cancel your return since you didn't use the other half of that round-trip ticket.

From: **Linda Bowman,** author of *Freebies (and More) for Folks Over 50.*

• ***Call hotels directly.*** To get the best deal, avoid the 800 numbers that lead to the central booking system. On-site reservations personnel may be able to find better rates that have not yet been listed on the central reservations system.

From: **Christopher Allen,** author of *Passport to Discount Travel.*

• ***Arrange to give lectures on a cruise.*** You can get a discount, or even a free ticket, if you use your expertise to entertain fellow passengers. Simply send out queries to various cruise lines describing your qualifications.

From: **Diane Warner,** author of *How to Have a Great Retirement on a Limited Budget.*

TAKE PICTURES FOR LESS...

• ***Buy low-cost, store-brand film.*** Retail chains such as Target and Kmart sell 35mm film by 3M Company and other high-quality manufacturers. *Cost:* 25% less than Kodak or Fuji.

From: **Lucy H. Hedrick,** a Greenwich, CT, time-management consultant and author of *365 Ways to Save Money.*

NEIGHBORS CAN HELP YOU SAVE...

• ***Share tasks, tools and time.*** If you think ahead, you can save a great deal by organizing exchanges and bargaining co-ops with friends and neighbors.

EXAMPLES: You can buy the electric drill, a neighbor can buy the leaf-blower. Or agree to baby-sit in exchange for help with chores. When you contract for services—such as lawn care, carpet cleaning, window washing or driveway resurfacing—coordinate with neighbors and negotiate a group discount.

From: **Mary Hunt,** author of *The Complete Cheapskate.*

• ***Cut down on wasted food.*** The average American wastes 15% of the food he/she buys. It simply gets thrown out. If you spend $500 a month on groceries, that adds up to $75 a month...$900 a year.

Buy items in the quantities you will really use. A gallon of spaghetti sauce may have a better unit price per ounce, but if you toss half of it because it gets moldy, then you've wasted more than you've saved.

From: **Rochelle LaMotte McDonald,** author of *How to Pinch a Penny Until it Screams.*

MEMORIAL SOCIETIES...

• ***Save when a loved one dies.*** The average funeral costs $5,000, but it doesn't have to. Join a local Memorial Society for a fee of about $25. These groups can negotiate funerals that cost much less. A no-frills package can cost as little as $1,000.

HOW: These nonprofit, volunteer organizations negotiate packages in advance with funeral directors and crematoriums, and provide free preplanning material.

MORE INFORMATION: Funeral & Memorial Societies of America, Box 10, Hinesburg, Vermont 05461. 800-765-0107.

From: **Amy Dacyczyn,** author of *The Tighwad Gazette.*

WHAT DO YOU HAVE ON TAP?...

• ***Water—drink more of it.*** First of all, it's good for you—you're supposed to drink eight glasses a day. You'll save a bundle on fruit juice, soft drinks, coffee and tea.

MORE SAVINGS: Buy frozen juices rather than those that are ready to drink.

From: **Mary Hunt,** author of *The Complete Cheapskate.*

■

SAVE THOUSANDS OF DOLLARS ON GROCERIES EVERY YEAR

Source: **Phil Lempert,** a food industry expert and inveterate supermarket shopper. He is author of *Phil Lempert's Supermarket Shopping and Value Guide.* Contemporary Books.

With more than 35,000 different products on most supermarket shelves, there's no reason to keep switching supermarkets to save money. Here's how to get the most from your supermarket of choice...

• ***Look for the best preferred-shopper program—and save $300.*** You can save $300 a year or more by consistently taking advantage of a supermarket's preferred-shopper program.

• Frequent-shopper programs issue a membership card or number that is used to electronically track the products you purchase. You accumulate points that can be redeemed for discounts, dollar awards or free products.

• Front-end electronic marketing programs are similar to frequent-shopper programs, but rewards are based on the amount spent.

• Purchase-triggered coupon programs, also called purchase-activated coupon programs, issue coupons at the checkout register that are good for future purchases at that particular store. The coupons are "triggered" by the purchases you have just made.

• Instant electronic discounts are also called "paperless coupons." Customers who use their membership cards at the checkout register automatically receive discounts on products that have been identified in mailers or by signs on the shelves. Some stores offer customers discounts at local businesses, entries in contests and other electronic rewards.

• ***Meet the store manager and/or customer service manager.*** Be sure to tell him/her that you are a regular customer, mention what you like about the store and suggest improvements. **ASK THE FOLLOWING QUESTIONS...**

• What are the best times to shop here? The worst?

• What are your biggest sale items?

• What day do weekly sales begin?

• Can I get an advance copy of your newspaper and circular ads and a schedule of in-store sales, product samplings and promotional events?

• How do I join your frequent-shopper program? Is there a fee? Will you waive it? (Usually the answer is *yes.*)

• ***Use coupons—and save $300.*** If you use just ten manufacturers' coupons a week, at an average of 60 cents each, you will save more than $300 a year.

• ***Buy store brands—and save $2,000.*** If you currently spend $135 to $140 a week on groceries, you can expect to save *more than $2,000 a year* by switching to store-brand products.

• ***Outsmart supermarket display techniques.*** Don't fall for these common supermarket display tricks...

• Placing the highest-priced items at eye level.

• Piling up end-of-aisle displays with products that are close to their expiration date, but are not necessarily on sale.

• Grouping products to provoke impulse buying, like chips, dips and soft drinks.

• Making attractive arrangements of delicious precut fruits or salad items that are far more expensive than the unsliced versions.

• Creating an "international" cheese table or deli display when the same prepackaged products are available in the dairy case for much less.

• Placing staple items, such as milk, in the back of the store, forcing you to walk past the rest of the merchandise.

• ***Stick to your list—and save $300.*** Always shop with a list and control your impulse buys for an easy savings of $300 a year. I limit myself to three impulse purchases per shopping trip, but otherwise stick to my list. This guarantees that I always have fun while I'm shopping—but I never exceed my budget.

■

ON-LINE SHOPPING TRAP

Source: **Diane Rosener,** editor and publisher, *A Penny Saved,* Box 3471, Omaha 68103.

Often-overlooked cost of shopping on-line: Shipping costs. Since anything you purchase must be sent to you, shipping charges can eat significantly into advertised cost savings.

EXAMPLE: A $13.95 book advertised on-line for $8.37—a 40% saving—costs $3.95 to ship. The total cost is therefore $12.32—a discount of only 12%. You would likely get an even better deal at a local discount bookstore.

ALSO: The shipping prices that you are quoted on-line are for regular-speed shipments. If you were to need faster delivery, the costs incurred would be even higher.

■

LARRY ROTH'S SIMPLE SECRETS OF LIVING THE GOOD LIFE FOR A LOT LESS

Source: **Larry Roth,** publisher of *Living Cheap News,* 7232 Belleview Ave., 2nd fl., Kansas City, MO 64114. He is editor of *The Simple Life,* an anthology of articles on frugal living. Berkley.

A few years ago, while I was industriously climbing the corporate ladder, I congratulated myself that my salary had increased fivefold during my 20-year career.

But then I realized that a new car had gone up in price sixfold during that period and my housing costs had increased more than 11 times! I was succeeding all the way to the poorhouse.

I decided I had to remove myself from the fast track and live frugally and follow in the footsteps of my grandparents—immigrants with low-skill jobs who nevertheless managed to join the American middle class, owning their own home and two Packards.

Here are the secrets of enjoying all of life's pleasures cheaply...

DOWNSIZE WISELY...

• ***Avoid debt.*** You're not getting anything from the interest you pay on credit cards, for example. Pay off all outstanding debt as soon as you can and *never* take on more.

• ***Don't leave town.*** Many retirees rush to relocate to Florida, Arizona or another Sunbelt paradise, only to find they've left their lives behind. A very expensive mistake, they eventually come running back, paying for *two* costly moves.

• ***Move into a smaller place.*** Just because you stay in the same area doesn't mean that you have to stay in the same house. Often, after you retire you don't want to keep up a large property.

WHAT TO DO: Find a smaller house or an apartment in your home town. The Taxpayer Relief Act of 1997 allows you to sell your house tax free, as long as your profit is $500,000 or less—$250,000 if you're single—and you owned and used the house as your principal residence for two out of five years before the sale.

Use some of the money to buy a new home and put the balance in income-producing investments.

A smaller home, you will be happy to discover, is a lot less expensive to operate.

• ***Pick a money-saving location for your retirement villa.*** *Prime places:* A house or an apartment near public transportation will allow you to get by with only one car—or none. You'll save money on insurance, inspections, maintenance, etc.

Or choose a home that's close to a public library. You'll save on books and have access to videos (no more movie admissions to pay), CDs, events, displays, etc.

DINE AT A DISCOUNT...

• ***Eat with the "early birds."*** Many restaurants offer dinner specials before 6 pm. Beat the crowds and save money.

In fact, you can eat like an *earlier* bird, by going for a late lunch when you're in the mood for a restaurant meal. At most restaurants, the lunch menu is much cheaper than the dinner menu— for the same food!

MORE SAVINGS: If you go to a restaurant for lunch, order more than you expect to eat. *Strategy:* Fill up at the salad bar and take your entree home for dinner.

• ***Ask for discounts.*** Many merchants offer lower prices to seniors. Always ask. There's no charge for inquiring. The worst that can happen is that you won't get a discount.

You may even get a better deal on your property taxes. It's worth a call to city hall to find out.

• ***Super-shop.*** Now that you have the time, compare supermarket prices in the newspapers and buy only items that are on sale—ideally, with a coupon. Stock up when staples are on sale. You might buy $50 worth of nonperishables one week—and then almost nothing for the next two weeks.

• ***Thrift-shop.*** Thrift shops often have great bargains, including half-price days and senior discounts.

• ***Late-shop.*** You can pick up amazing bargains at estate sales, especially on the last day of the sale when "everything must go."

• ***Never buy new if used will do.*** Secondhand items may be in excellent condition, yet much cheaper. Scan local classified listings, supermarket bulletin boards, etc. Garage sales and auctions frequently offer outstanding values.

When you buy through such informal channels you may not have to pay sales tax.

PATIENCE IS A VIRTUE...

• ***Travel at the last minute.*** Often, cruise ships and airlines are willing to offer incredible fares to fill up space that otherwise would be empty. Try a few travel agents to find one who'll help you. Or get a personal computer with a modem and track down your own discounts on the Internet.

• ***Call late.*** Make long-distance calls after 11 pm when phone rates generally go down. Or call on weekends. *Caution:* Rates may jump back up on Sunday at 5 pm.

SURE THINGS...

• ***Be sure about your insurance.*** You may not need life insurance —if your kids are independent and your spouse will be protected by your pension, IRA, etc. If so, you can stop paying premiums on any term insurance and cash in any whole-life policies.

Look hard at your health insurance, too. It is usually a big expense for retirees. Rather than buy a Medigap policy, which is probably pricey, do your homework to find an inexpensive Medicare HMO with well-regarded, conveniently located doctors.

Make certain that your auto insurer knows that you're retired. Chances are you'll get a "low mileage" premium. If your present insurer won't offer you a discount, find one that will.

• ***Buy bonds.*** The interest you receive from these investments will bolster your income. Assuming you earn 5%, every $10,000 you invest will yield $500 per year, more than $40 a month. And your principal will be available in case of emergency.

■

CREDIT CARD TRAP

Source: **Robert McKinley,** president of RAM Research and publisher of *Card-Trak,* a monthly guide to the best credit card deals, Box 1700, Frederick, MD 21702.

Beware of credit card offers that say *Fixed low rate!* or *Not an introductory rate!*

PROBLEM: Despite the wording, the low rate is not guaranteed forever. Under federal law, card issuers can jack up the rate with as little as 15 days notice. And—many card issuers offer low rates for the first year and then hike them skyward in the second. *Also:* There may be other hidden traps. *Example:* A "punitive rate" of 20% or more for making a single late payment...a 20- to 25-day grace period (the time before interest begins accruing), compared with the industry average of 25 to 30...interest calculated on the costly *two-cycle average* daily balance instead of a single cycle.

SELF-DEFENSE: Always read the fine print.

■

DON'T PAY FOR UNLISTED NUMBER

Source: **Melodie Moore,** editor, *Tightwad Living,* Box 629, Burgin, KY 40310.

Save the cost of an unlisted phone number by simply listing your phone under a name other than your common name—such as your middle name. People trying to find your name in the phone book won't be able to do so. And whenever you get a call asking for the bogus name, you'll know it is an unsolicited sales call.

■

LOWER LONG-DISTANCE BILL

Source: **Bob Spangler,** deputy chief, Common Carrier Bureau, Federal Communications Commission, Washington, DC.

To lower your monthly long-distance bill: Call your long-distance carrier and ask it to calculate which of its plans is best for your current calling pattern.

The big three long-distance companies—AT&T, MCI and Sprint—together control 85% of the market, and each has numerous discount plans available. While it costs nothing to ask—and usually nothing to get into a plan—many long-distance customers use no special discount plan at all.

IMPORTANT: Each time your calling pattern changes, go through the process again.

■

2
THE INVESTMENT GAME

HOW AN 8TH-GRADE STUDENT INVESTMENT CLUB MADE 10,000% PROFIT!

Source: **Jim Bedrava,** 8th-grade English and social studies teacher at Port Huron South School in Port Huron, MI. He is adviser to the Port Huron South Eagles Investment Team, which won The 1997 CNBC/MCI Student Stock Tournament.

In the final three months of last year, the eighth-grade students in the investment club I coach earned a paper profit of 10,000% in The CNBC/MCI Student Stock Tournament...and won.

We turned $10,000 into $1 million, though these returns resulted from nuances specific to the contest. **EXAMPLES...**

- ***The club invested imaginary money.***
- ***There were no brokerage commissions or taxes to pay.***
- ***Since our only goal was to finish first, we took many more risks than if we had used real money***—sometimes trading several times in a day. We did this without leverage.

Along the way we learned many lessons about finding great stocks—lessons that can help any investor...

- ***Cast a broad net for ideas.*** Investing in companies that affect your life positively is a good way to find great stocks.

EXAMPLE: One of our best stock picks was Yahoo! Inc., a company that allows users to access Internet sites quickly. My students and I used its Web sites a great deal when researching stocks.

You should also look for companies in industries with which most investors are unlikely to interact regularly.

HELPFUL: We taped many CNBC programs, such as "Power Lunch" and "Squawk Box." We also read *The Wall Street Journal* and tracked Reuters (http://biz.yahoo.com/finance) and Business Wire (http://www.businesswire.com) on-line.

The financial media provided us with terrific leads into companies and their top executives. If we saw a CEO being interviewed on TV who was impressive, we would look into his/her company.

The Internet also was a terrific source of information. We would check Reuters and Business Wire every hour. When a bit of corporate news caught our eye—perhaps because the company was rumored to be an acquisition target or it was reporting record earnings—we would research the company's financial health and prospects.

• ***Research stocks fast—without spending a dime.*** We didn't use the Internet just to find investment ideas. We used it to look into stocks that we were considering for our portfolio.

Since we were a public school earning imaginary profits, we didn't have real money to throw around subscribing to expensive research tools. But we found just about everything we could hope for—from current valuations to historical charts—*free* on the Internet.

EXAMPLE: Quarterly and annual reports can be obtained through Yahoo! (http://quote.yahoo.com) or Infoseek (http://www.infoseek.com).

Financial documents can be complex, but we learned that it isn't necessary to understand everything in them to size up a stock. We paid attention to the *outlook* section of the annual report. It details the company's plans for the coming year. We liked companies whose outlooks sounded ambitious and exciting.

We also scanned the financial documents to see what they said about the company's...

• Competitors. We avoided companies that seemed nervous or apprehensive about rivals.

• Earnings. We favored companies whose earnings were growing and beat estimates.

• New products. We looked for companies that announced they had many new products in the pipeline.

• ***Look at the big picture.*** We focused our efforts on industries that seemed so promising that most stocks in that sector probably would be dragged upward. And they were.

Two of our favorite sectors were pharmaceuticals and telecommunications.

REASON: People always are going to get sick, so medical-related stocks are somewhat recession-proof. And the demand for faster, more efficient telecommunications will continue to grow as the technology becomes more affordable.

• Pharmaceuticals. Large companies with diversified product lines were especially attractive to us. Small pharmaceutical firms with only one or two major drugs can be very risky. A lot of things can go wrong with any single drug—a new competitor...failure to get approval from the Food and Drug Administration (FDA)...or lapsing patent protection.

We like companies with products in the pipeline that target widespread conditions. A baldness treatment or breast cancer drug offers much greater sales potential than even the most successful breakthrough for a rare disease.

• Telecommunications. We believe that this sector has the potential to be the next huge growth area, much as technology was in the 1980s.

• ***Look at a company's foreign exposure...***and imagine how that exposure will affect its profits. We have stayed away from a lot of technology stocks because many of them have significant operations in Asia. That makes them vulnerable to the problems of that region.

On the other hand, retailers such as Pier 1 Imports and Wal-Mart could find that the prices of the goods they're importing from Asia are dropping, which would boost their profits.

In the airline industry, fuel prices have a considerable impact on profits. They might rise or fall significantly, depending on the political situation in the Middle East.

• ***Look for reasons why the timing to buy is right.*** Market timing is not a smart approach for long-term investors. It's better to buy the stocks of good companies and hang onto them for as long as possible. But it's still important to buy shares at the right moment. Often, a big gain in a stock will be related to an acquisition, merger, higher-than-expected earnings report or—in the case of pharmaceutical companies—FDA approval of a key drug.

These things are tough for a small investor to determine in advance. By following Reuters and Business Wire on-line, as well as financial TV programs, we were able to stay on top of these developments.

EXAMPLE: We've found that prior to a major computer industry trade show is a good time to invest in computer companies. Technology companies like to announce news at those shows. Business Wire includes a site that lists industry trade shows (http://www.businesswire.com/tradeshow).

• ***Compare your opinion with those of the experts.*** Our final step before buying shares is to make as certain as possible that there isn't something we overlooked about the company.

HELPFUL: Through Yahoo! on-line, we were able to find out consensus opinion of Wall Street analysts on the stock.

If the consensus rating was low—there were more *holds* or *sells* than *buys*—we would do more research to determine the reason or choose another stock.

■

SIMPLE PROGRAM FOR BUILDING A SAFE, DIVERSIFIED PORTFOLIO...AT ANY AGE

Source: **Jonathan Pond,** president, Financial Planning Information Inc., Nine Galen St., Watertown, MA 02472. He is the host of *Your Financial Future,* a public television series and author of *4 Easy Steps to Successful Investing.* Avon Books.

The popular myth that when you are about to retire you've got to make major changes in the way you invest is just plain *wrong!*

Assuming you've invested wisely during your working years, all that's required for retirees and preretirees is some fine-tuning.

As you know, mutual funds give you professional management and diversification at a low cost. If you've become a more sophisticated investor, you can add individual stocks and bonds to give yourself greater control over the timing of capital gains taxation and other factors.

ALLOCATION...

It's important to figure out how much of the total you have to invest should go into *stock funds*...and how much into *bond funds.* I've reduced this to a fairly simple calculation...

• ***Aggressive portfolio allocation...***for those who are still far enough from retirement to be comfortable with risk. Subtract your age from 120. The resulting amount is the approximate percentage you should put into stock funds.

EXAMPLE: A 40-year-old might invest about 80% (120–40 = 80) in stock funds and 20% in bond funds.

• ***Moderate portfolio allocation...***for those closer to retirement. They can arrive at a more suitable allocation by subtracting their age from 110. Put that amount in stock funds, and the rest in bond funds.

EXAMPLE: A 65-year-old investor recognizes the need to continue investing for growth as well as income. He might put 45% (110–65 = 45) in stock funds and 55% in bond funds.

• ***Conservative portfolio allocation...***for those who aren't comfortable with the ups and downs of the stock market. Subtract your age from 100. The resulting amount is the approximate percentage that should go into stocks. The rest should go in bonds.

EXAMPLE: A 53-year-old woman knows she needs growth, but is skittish about the stock market. She might put 47% of her money in stock funds (100–53 = 47) and 53% in bond funds.

As your age increases, you will gradually invest more money in bonds—and less in stocks. But you don't have to change your allocation every year. These are not rigid standards, but merely guidelines. However, they should be viewed as *minimums*. Even when you are over 70, continue to keep at least 30% of your long-term investment money in stocks because you will still need growth to help you keep up with inflation during the rest of your life.

DIVERSIFICATION...

The next step is deciding how much of your investment portfolio to put in various fund categories.

• ***Preretirees—those within ten years of retirement...***

STOCK FUNDS: 20% growth...40% growth and income...20% small company...20% international.

BOND FUNDS: 20% long-term bonds...20% short/intermediate-term municipal bonds...15% long-term US government bonds... 15% short/intermediate-term US government bonds...15% long-term corporate...15% short/intermediate-term corporate.

For prudent diversification you need different types of bonds *and* different maturities.

• ***Retirees—a slight shift to more conservative and higher-income-producing categories...***

STOCK FUNDS: 15% growth...55% growth and income...15% small company...15% international.

BOND FUNDS: 15% long-term municipal...25% short/intermediate-term municipal...10% long-term US government...20% short/intermediate-term US government...10% long-term corporate...20% short/intermediate corporate.

You may want to add real estate funds (REITs, *not* limited partnerships).

You don't need much of a cash or money market emergency fund since it only takes a few days to sell mutual funds.

PICKING FUNDS...

Next, you need to pick a solid mutual fund portfolio and then monitor the funds regularly to check on their performance relative to other funds in their category.

MY RULE: Don't sell a fund until it has underperformed its peers' average for two consecutive years.

The process of selecting good funds may seem overwhelming, but there's a lot of help out there. If you use a paid adviser, be sure to ask why he/she is high on a given fund.

BETTER: Go to the library and check out the fund in mutual fund monitoring services such as *The Value Line Mutual Fund Survey* or *Morningstar.* Look for funds ranked one or two in Value Line or those with an overall ranking of four or five stars in Morningstar.

Read all you can about mutual funds in the major financial newspapers and magazines.

VERY HELPFUL: The Friday edition of *The Wall Street Journal,* which has detailed coverage and ranking on fund performance over one, three and five years.

Personally, I won't invest in a fund that hasn't been around for five years. Choose mostly top-rated funds.

FINE-TUNING...

Periodically rebalancing your investment allocation can transform very good investment results into *excellent* investment results.

REASON: Rebalancing forces you to do the right thing—that is sell some stocks after a big run-up and put more money into bonds.

About every six months, add up your investments by categories and see how the allocation has changed due to market fluctuations.

You should also rebalance after a major change in stock prices (more than 10%) or interest rates (more than 1%).

Calculate the current percentage in each category of stocks and bonds and compare that with the target allocation you chose, noting how much you'd have to add to or subtract from each category to get back to the original balance.

CAUTION: Consider tax consequences and transaction costs as well as the time and difficulty of making these changes. You may decide to live with the imbalance for another six months or so.

■

401(K)S...AND COMPANY STOCK

Source: **Laurence I. Foster, CPA/PFS,** tax partner, personal financial planning practice, KPMG Peat Marwick LLP, 345 Park Ave., New York 10154.

New studies show that the average employee has as much as a third of his/her 401(k) and other retirement savings invested in shares of the employer company's stock. That may be too heavy a concentration.

It may be unwise, even though the stock may be purchased at a discount...is often matched by company contributions...and may result in some tax benefits at retirement. Remember that your salary and your health insurance are also dependent on that one company. It may be better to put most of your 401(k) money into more diverse investments.

■

ALL ABOUT THE ROTH IRA

Source: **Leonard J. Witman, Esq.,** an expert on the subject of estate planning for retirement benefits. He is tax partner in the law firm of Witman, Stadtmauer & Michaels, PA, 26 Columbia Tpk., Florham Park, NJ 07932, and adjunct professor of law at Seton Hall Law School, Newark, NJ.

You can now have a new kind of IRA—a Roth IRA—that can give you *tax-free* retirement income.

Everyone who falls within the law's income limits should consider setting up a Roth IRA. But to make the best use of a Roth, you'll have to closely coordinate investment planning, tax planning and estate planning. What you need to know...

BASIC FEATURES OF ROTH IRAS...

- ***Contributions to Roth IRAs are not tax deductible.***
- ***Funds held in a Roth IRA for at least five years*** can be withdrawn tax free after age 59½.
- ***There are no mandatory withdrawals from Roth IRAs,*** as there are from regular IRAs at age 70½.
- ***You can withdraw your own contributions from a Roth IRA at any time*** tax free and penalty free.
- ***You can make a full $2,000 annual contribution to a Roth IRA*** so long as your Adjusted Gross Income (AGI) is under $150,000 (joint) or $95,000 (single).

• ***Being covered by an employer's qualified retirement plan won't make you ineligible*** for a Roth IRA.

• ***You can convert your conventional IRAs into Roths*** in a year your AGI isn't over $100,000.

• ***When you convert to a Roth IRA,*** you owe tax on the taxable income from the money you withdraw from your regular IRA to put in the Roth IRA.

MAJOR ADVANTAGES OF ROTHS...

• ***Tax-free build-up and withdrawal.*** Distributions from regular IRAs are taxed at normal income tax rates, up to 39.6%. But—distributions from Roths can be tax free. So, you can make high-growth investments and pay zero tax.

This benefit is greatest if investments grow in Roth IRAs at high rates for many years.

• ***Flexibility.*** Unlike regular IRAs, you can...

• Take *early* tax-free and penalty-free withdrawals of your own $2,000 contributions to Roth IRAs at any time—even before age 59½, or...

• *Delay* withdrawals from Roth IRAs until after you reach age 70½ to earn more tax-free compound returns.

$2,000 A YEAR IN A ROTH...

Making annual $2,000 contributions to a Roth IRA can be better than contributing to a regular IRA because you can use a Roth IRA as a flexible tax-free savings account. You can take funds out early—or leave them in the Roth IRA longer than you could in a regular IRA.

OPPORTUNITY: The fact that you don't ever have to take withdrawals means you can use a Roth IRA to fund bequests to heirs.

If a young child inherits a Roth IRA, it may be possible that tax-free compounding of investment returns over the decades of a young child's life and future tax-free status for withdrawals can have a combined effect so that even a modest amount left to the child provides great financial benefits.

PLANNING: If you are covered by an employer's qualified retirement plan, such as a 401(k), make contributions to that plan first—at least as far as your employer makes matching contributions to your account. Make a $2,000 contribution to a Roth IRA on top of that.

Contributing to a Roth IRA is more advantageous than to a non-deductible conventional IRA.

PROBLEMATIC FOR SENIORS...

In addition to contributing $2,000 each year to a new Roth IRA, you can also convert some or all of your old IRAs into Roth IRAs.

IMPORTANT: Often it will *not* be advantageous for persons over 50 to convert their regular IRAs to Roth IRAs. Problems with Roth IRAs for seniors...

• ***Smaller benefits.*** The benefits of a Roth IRA are maximized when it earns high returns for many years. But persons in or near retirement will have their money in a Roth IRA for fewer years, and may invest conservatively—thus reducing the benefits.

• ***Big tax bills.*** Seniors with regular IRAs that have large amounts of investment buildup will incur a big tax bill on conversion.

Even if the tax is spread over four years, the money to pay it must come from *somewhere...*

• If it comes from the IRA, it will seriously reduce its value.

• If it comes from other investments, the benefit of converting will be partially offset by the loss of earnings on those investments.

• If it comes from spending money, it will affect your standard of living.

• ***State taxes.*** A large state tax bill may apply to the conversion. While the IRS will let you pay the federal tax due over four years, each state has its own rules—and some may not allow this break.

• ***Complicates retiring to a tax-haven state.*** If you plan to move to a no-tax or low-tax state after retiring in the next few years, you will reduce the value of receiving tax-free income from the Roth IRA without reducing the cost of the conversion now. But you'll pay the high-tax cost of converting to your present high-tax-state's revenue department.

• ***May open your IRA money to creditors' claims.*** A Roth IRA may not receive protection against creditors in your state. While most states give regular IRAs some protection against creditor claims, some states do not give the same protection to Roth IRAs—though hopefully those states will amend their laws.

CAUTION: Before going ahead with a Roth IRA, check to see if it is protected against creditor claims in your state.

BOTTOM LINE...

For all these reasons, converting regular IRAs to Roth IRAs may be less attractive for seniors than for younger IRA owners.

However, the only way to be sure whether or not converting regular IRAs to Roth IRAs will be good for you is to run through the numbers with a professional tax or financial adviser.

OPTION: Convert only *some* of your regular IRAs into Roth IRAs—enough to increase your flexibility in making tax-free withdrawals, and to fund bequests to grandchildren. Leave the rest in regular IRAs, to avoid the full tax that would be due if all were converted to Roth IRAs.

■

SENIORS AND ROTH IRAS

Source: **Stephen J. Krass, Esq.,** senior partner, Krass & Lund, PC, 419 Park Ave. S., New York 10016, and author of *The Pension Answer Book.* Panel Publishers.

The new Roth IRA will be better for seniors than conventional IRAs. *Why:* Unlike a regular IRA, you can continue contributing to a Roth IRA after age 70½ as long as you have earned income...*and* you do not have to begin taking mandatory distributions from a Roth IRA at age 70½...*and* after age 59½, distributions of earnings on funds that have been held in a Roth IRA for at least five years are *totally tax free.* The result—you can use a Roth IRA to generate tax-free investment returns for as long in life as you like.

■

3
MONEY MANAGEMENT

HOW TO PREPARE A BUDGET THAT YOU CAN BE HAPPY WITH

Source: **Ray Martin, CFP,** a vice president at State Street Global Advisors, Boston, and contributing correspondent to NBC's *Today* show. He is author of *The Rookie's Guide to Money Management*. Random House.

Anyone can create a plan that controls spending and boosts savings. The key is knowing where your money goes—knowing exactly what is coming in and what is going out.

WHERE TO START...

• ***For the next two months, keep track of all of your expenses.*** If you are like most people, what's going out doesn't equal what's coming in, but don't be ashamed of it. The first step is to build awareness.

• List your essential expenses. These are items you cannot do without—rent or mortgage, insurance premiums, commuting costs, child care, food, loan payments, clothing (including laundry and dry cleaning) and utilities (use a monthly average, but don't underestimate).

• List your everyday "extras" including entertainment (cable TV, movies, CDs, video rentals, dining out, sports or theater tickets, books, etc.), nonessential clothing, expensive haircuts, etc.

• List your big yearly luxuries: Vacations...holiday gifts...a new car in three years, etc. Attach dollar amounts to each.

• Calculate an amount for annual savings. Ideally, most people should save at least 10% of their *gross* yearly income. The amount may seem high, given all of your other expenses, but it really isn't once you get spending in order.

• ***Calculate your annual household income,*** including paychecks, bonuses and any interest and dividends you receive from investments. Divide this total amount by 12 to get your average monthly income.

• ***Convert quarterly and annual expenses into monthly amounts.*** You will probably find that your expenses exceed your monthly net income. About 75% of Americans are in the same boat.

HOW TO CUT...

• ***Use a money-management software program.*** While there is nothing wrong with a sharp pencil and a spiral notebook, I find that managing finances electronically saves two valuable commodities—time and money.

Most programs are easy to use and print your income and expense report at the touch of a button.

MY FAVORITE EASY-TO-USE MONEY-MANAGEMENT PROGRAMS: *Quicken* or *Microsoft Money*. ***Cost:*** $30 to $40.

• ***Keep a log of absolutely everything you spend.*** The more often you make yourself aware of your expenses, the more likely you will be to stick to your spending plan.

I guarantee you'll be surprised by how much money slips through your fingers.

EXAMPLE: The $2.20 spent on gourmet coffee every morning becomes about $48 a month...$576 a year...and more than $11,520 over 20 years. If you invested that money at 8%, it would be $26,313 in 20 years.

Is that too much for coffee? It depends on what's truly important to you, and whether you can live with a cup of coffee that costs half as much.

• ***Curb the splurges.*** They really add up. You don't have to eliminate them entirely, but you do have to find cheaper ways of enjoying them. These splurges include eating out...buying casual weekend clothing...video rentals...CDs...home furnishings...stereo and home-theater equipment.

• ***Find ways to trim your necessities.*** Most people spend more than they should on necessities.

EXAMPLES: Everyone needs a credit card, but your debt can be trimmed by switching to a card with a lower rate.

Life insurance is a must, but your premiums can be reduced if you shop around for another policy that offers the same coverage for a lower premium.

PUT IT IN WRITING...

Once you have juggled the numbers so your income is more than what is needed to cover your expenses, you have created a blueprint for financial success. The goal now is to find ways to make sure you stick with it.

If the plan gets derailed by an unexpected event (health problem, loss of job) or an expected one (a new child, new home), sit down with your partner and redo the plan.

If you made it work once, you can make it work again.

■

SHREWD MONEY LESSONS FROM THOSE FANTASTICALLY FRUGAL FARMERS

Source: **Jim Jorgensen,** who grew up on a farm and now is a nationwide radio host and editor of *It's Your Money,* 118 Camino Pablo, Orinda, CA 94563. He is author of several books, including *Money Lessons for a Lifetime.* Dearborn.

When I was growing up in the 1940s, my family moved from Omaha to a small farming community in central California.

Now I am a financial planner, but in my 30 years in this business, few people have had a more lasting effect on my life than the savvy farmers I knew in my youth.

Here are the financial secrets of farmers that anyone can use today...

• ***If you can't afford to pay cash, buy it used.*** The richest farmers I knew tried to avoid borrowing whenever possible. The idea of paying two or three times the original purchase price in interest payments over several years appalled them.

Whenever they could, they'd try to coax a few more months or years out of a piece of equipment by repairing it. If the machinery was not salvageable, they would replace it—usually with a newer but not necessarily brand new piece of equipment.

I follow this practice today, even though I can afford to buy new. It saves me thousands of dollars on cars, as well as clothes and furniture. **EXAMPLES...**

• I always drive a Cadillac, but I'm never the car's first owner. I always buy a model that has been around for 18 to 24 months, when the cost has dropped by thousands of dollars.

• My wife and I recently bought a chair for our bedroom. It is a fine piece of furniture, but we got it at an upscale consignment shop. We paid only $180—not the $500 we would have spent if we bought it new.

• ***Be conservative with your investments.*** Most of the successful farmers I knew were not big financial risk takers. They worked hard for the money they accumulated.

When they invested, they stuck with the bluest of the blue-chip stocks. They bought only companies with good track records of earnings and histories of paying steadily increasing dividends.

Rather than take the dividends, these farmers reinvested the payout in additional shares of the companies' stocks. After decades of squirreling away extra cash in tried-and-true companies and reinvesting the dividends, these farmers saw their net worth swell to 10 to 20 times their original investment.

• ***Buy real estate—or real estate funds.*** Many of the farmers I grew up with became rich by purchasing and holding on to property.

They became well-acquainted with what was available through their agriculture activities, and when something good came on the market, they'd snap it up immediately.

They would quietly add parcel after parcel to their holdings, and when it came time for them to retire, they were able to sell off some of their real estate at a handsome profit.

These days it's hard to find good properties at reasonable prices, and the appreciation that everyone took for granted in the 1980s is no longer a sure thing.

HELPFUL: Consider investing 10% to 20% of your portfolio in a mutual fund that restricts its holdings to Real Estate Investment Trusts (REITs)—and firms that specialize in developing and managing commercial and residential property.

These funds are the only way I know for individual investors to buy property and have liquidity. You only have to put a few thousand dollars down and can invest as little as $100 or so a month after that, in order to build a good portfolio.

Plus, you get an income stream from rental receipts that can help cushion the rest of your portfolio in a downturn.

• ***Make compounding work for you.*** Once you save a little money and invest it, that money will begin to generate more income through dividend or interest payments. By reinvesting those dividends and interest, and adding them to your original savings, you will generate even more money. This is the process of compounding...and the earlier you start, the more powerful it will be.

EXAMPLE: One penny-pinching farmer saved just a few bucks a day and retired wealthy. Beginning at age 35, he invested $200 a month in good growth-stock funds and continued to do so until he reached age 65. Over this 30-year period, he invested a total of only $72,000.

Yet his retirement nest egg grew to more than $1 million. The lesson is that the other $928,000—or more than 90% of his retirement nest egg—was created through compounding and consisted of money he never contributed in the first place.

■

JUST SAY "NO" TO DEBT

Source: **Luther Gatling,** president of Budget & Credit Counseling Services, a nonprofit consumer advocacy organization, 55 Fifth Ave., New York 10003.

The early part of a new year is a great time to put yourself on a "debt diet." Here are some strategies for keeping credit- and store-card balances down...

• ***Steer clear of zero-interest deferred-payment options.*** These are the deals that allow you to delay paying for a purchase for up to one year, interest-free.

TRAP: If you miss the payment deadline, all the finance charges accrued since the date of the purchase will be due. Usually, these charges are 22%—and sometimes more.

• ***Save money by asking merchants if they are planning to discount big-ticket items.*** Shopping for a new stereo or refrigerator? Ask if the item will be going on sale in the near future. Most retailers will answer you truthfully.

• ***Never pay for groceries with a credit card.*** It's an easy way to pump up your debt load. Also avoid charging utility and telephone bills, rent and house payments. These should be budgeted as fixed expenses and paid for by check.

• ***Leave home without it.*** If you are a plastic junkie, keep one credit card in your wallet for emergencies and put the others away. Always pay for small purchases by check or cash only.

• ***Cancel cards you don't need.*** The more cards you own, the more you're likely to overspend. Three is all you ever need. Cancel the rest.

IMPORTANT: To protect your credit rating, have the card company inform the credit agencies that you canceled the account. Tell the company to report the account as "closed by consumer." To make sure this is done, check your credit report once a year.

• ***Proceed very carefully when switching to low-interest cards.*** Before shifting high-interest debt to a card with a lower introductory rate, read the fine print on the membership agreement.

On some cards, the cheaper rate applies only to new purchases. Also, pay off all charges on a low-interest card quickly.

REASON: After the introductory period—usually six months—the rate may bump up to 18%...or even higher.

• ***Make sure you're credited for double payments.*** To make a double payment, send separate checks in two envelopes with a note requesting that one check be credited toward the following month.

• ***Give yourself a spending limit when buying gifts.*** Forget about finding the "perfect" gift for birthdays and anniversaries regardless of the cost. Instead, set a realistic budget before setting foot in a mall...and stick to it.

The person who receives your gift is likely to forget it long after you are still paying for it.

• ***Borrow against your mortgage to pay off existing credit card balances.*** It's a way of getting a low-interest loan so that you can quickly wipe out high-interest card balances. Also, you will be able to spread repayment out over the lifetime of your mortgage.

■

HOW TO GET OUT OF DEBT...FAST THE PROVEN STRATEGIES

Source: **David Masten,** president of Credit Insider, a fee-based service that helps consumers correct credit problems, 160 Fifth Ave., New York 10010. He is also publisher of *Credit Insider Magazine,* which teaches how to build, improve and repair credit and manage debt.

By paying only the minimum required on a large credit card bill, you will spend about 30 years paying off the balance. Here are shrewd ways to decrease your debt load in a lot shorter period of time...

• ***Transfer your balances to a card with a low standard rate.*** This is always the best first step—but *only* if you do it right and avoid the traps.

By switching to a card with a 9% variable or fixed interest rate, you can pay off a $10,000 debt in just a few years—if you pay the same monthly minimum you would have paid on your former 18% interest card.

IMPORTANT: Stick to cards that offer a low *standard* rate and low annual fee—and avoid cards with *introductory* rates.

Once attractive introductory rates expire, you often pay a rate that is similar to the former card's.

• ***Renegotiate your loan agreement.*** If your debt seems unmanageable—even at 9%—call your current card issuer to ask about setting up a resettlement policy.

The credit card industry is facing extremely high customer-default rates, and issuers are terrified of cardholders who are, or may soon be, over their heads in debt.

To avoid complete losses, many lending institutions have established little-known alternative repayment programs to handle "hard times" customers. **STEPS TO TAKE...**

• Negotiate to freeze your debt. Call your card company and request that it freeze your debt where it stands now. Then suggest that an alternative payment arrangement be set up.

A reasonable repayment schedule is any one that you can meet, whether it's $80 a month for ten years or $1,000 a month for three months. Any debt level, if delinquent, is enough leverage to get you what you want from the issuer.

You likely will meet some resistance to your request. If you've made minimum payments on the card's balance until now, your creditor may reasonably ask why you don't continue to do so.

Explain that freezing the amount owed combined with a new repayment schedule is the most ideal solution given your present financial situation.

If the issuer wants you to put together an accounting of your present debt/income situation to aid in its decision, politely refuse.

REASON: You are giving the issuer an opportunity to say your situation isn't dire enough for such a program—even though you may feel your financial situation is very tight.

BETTER: Politely but firmly tell the issuer's representative that you have already decided a new plan is needed, and that the company's analysis of your finances won't change your position.

If the person you are speaking to isn't willing to help, insist that you speak with someone who can negotiate such an agreement.

In the end, most creditors will make a deal with you because it's in their best interest.

• Get it in writing. Once the issuer agrees to a repayment plan, ask for a letter from the issuer outlining the terms. Be sure the deal includes a promise by the issuer not to report anything negative about your account to the credit bureaus, provided you make the agreed-upon payments on time.

If your creditor resists sending you a letter, suggest that you will put your understanding of the agreement in writing and send it by certified return-receipt mail, keeping a copy for your records.

You might even enclose a first payment, and state in your letter that cashing the check means the issuer has agreed to the new terms.

• Follow up with the credit bureaus. It is your responsibility to make sure the three credit bureaus—Equifax (800-685-1111), Experian (800-392-1122) and TransUnion (800-916-8800)—update your records.

Once your debt is paid off, make sure your card issuer is not reporting negative information about your account. You may need to follow up in 45 days with another copy of this same letter to ensure that the account status is actually changed.

The best way to ensure that no bad information will be reported after the debt is paid is to close the account.

• ***Borrow against real estate holdings or brokerage accounts.*** Both loans have an interest rate of about 9%—which is often lower than most credit cards.

• ***Sell CDs, stocks and other savings instruments.*** Weak-performing stocks and cash savings are good sources of money to pay off debt. ■

EASY WAYS TO BOOST INCOME

Source: **Stephen M. Pollan,** a lawyer in private practice and a financial adviser in New York. He is coauthor of *Starting Over: How to Change Careers or Start Your Own Business.* Warner Books.

There are two ways to raise the amount of money you have in the bank—get a raise, lower your expenses...or both.

STRATEGIES...

• ***Make yourself more valuable at work.*** Act as if every day were your first day on the job...

•Pay special attention to your attire and grooming.

•Smile...act enthusiastic and interested.

•Don't gossip.

•Become a walking "suggestion box."

•Become a student of your company and learn as much as you can about your industry.

•Arrive at work early. Make yourself an authority in your field of expertise.

Such behavior will be noticed and make you a "halo" employee. In the event of a downsizing, you'll be among the last to be let go.

OPPORTUNITY: Chat with your boss every three to six months to see how you're doing.

• ***Explore new career opportunities.*** If things aren't going well at work, look aggressively for something better. Be prepared—so that, if necessary, you can make your move before your company writes you off.

Many people avoid looking for work outside their current fields because they are paralyzed by fears that their skills are too specialized. *Reality:* Only rarely is this true. Most skills are highly transferable. Build bridges to fields outside your own so you can convince decision makers in those fields that you can do the job.

OPPORTUNITY: When seeking a job in a different field, target small companies first. They're more likely to take risks with people outside their industries.

• ***Reduce high-interest debt.*** If necessary, tap your emergency fund to pay off expensive loans such as credit card debt. If an emergency hits, you can always borrow to pay for it.

Refinance existing debts with cheaper money by borrowing against your home, retirement plan or life insurance policy.

Don't incur new credit card debt. Carry only one credit card, and pay off new charges every month.

• ***Make lifestyle changes to improve your financial position.***

• Dining out. Eat dinner at home, instead of restaurants, as often as possible. Bring your lunch to work.

• Gift-giving. Make your own gifts. It will save you money and may actually *enhance* friendships.

• Grocery shopping. Buy only what's on your list, use coupons, buy store brands and stock up during sales.

• Regular, but unnecessary, purchases. These add up over time—for example, cappuccino, bottled water and too many toys for your children.

OPPORTUNITY: Set a reasonable annual goal for reducing discretionary spending—such as 5% to 15%—*and live up to it.*

■

TO MAKE EXTRA MONEY

Source: **Jay Conrad Levinson** is author of *555 Ways to Earn Extra Money.* Henry Holt.

Test coach. Prepare students for tests either by teaching them the subject or showing them how to study...and how to relax during exams. Advertise your services on school bulletin boards.

EARNINGS: About $15 to $25 per hour.

• ***Trade show representative.*** Help convention exhibitors demonstrate products, greet customers, take tickets, etc.

Contact the convention and visitors bureau for a list of conventions and write to the organizers. Also offer your services direct to convention and show halls.

EARNINGS: Approximately $25 to $50 per day, or pay and commission.

• ***Reader for the vision impaired.*** Write offering your services to nursing homes, hospitals and senior citizen groups.

EARNINGS: About $5 to $10 per hour.

• ***Clipping newspaper articles.*** If you're a fast, efficient reader, consider working for clipping services. They subscribe to papers for you and send you lists of topics to search for. Check the *Yellow Pages* for clipping bureaus near you.

EARNINGS: Amounts vary around the country. About $7 per hour in New York State.

■

STRETCHING DUE DATES ON BILLS

Due dates on bills can be stretched—but not far—without risk. *Typical grace periods:* Telephone companies, eight days. Gas and electric utilities, ten days. Banks and finance companies, ten days.

Even after a late charge is imposed on an unpaid bill your credit rating should be safe for 30 days.

■

4

TAXPAYER VICTORIES

HOW TO KEEP YOUR SECRETS FROM THE IRS ...LEGALLY

Source: **Frederick W. Daily, Esq.,** a tax attorney based in San Francisco. He is author of *Stand Up to the IRS* and *Tax Savvy for Small Business.* Nolo Press.

The IRS probably doesn't know as much about you as you think it does. And if you know your rights, you may be able to prevent it from learning more about you than you want. To keep secrets from the IRS...

FUNDAMENTALS...

The first thing to realize is that the IRS is not the all powerful or all knowing agency many taxpayers fear it to be...

• ***IRS computer systems are obsolete.*** This makes it difficult for IRS agents to get information about you from the IRS's own files. If you are called for an audit, it's most likely the only information the auditor will have about you will be your tax return and information returns (W-2, 1099s, etc.) for the year in question.

RESULT: An IRS auditor who needs extra information to pursue an audit will have to get it from you. By not volunteering any information, you can contain your audit risk.

• ***You do not have to produce information just because an IRS auditor requests it.*** In the vast majority of cases, not responding to an auditor's request for information will simply result in the disallowance of the deduction to which the information relates—and nothing worse than that.

STRATEGY: It can be the better part of valor to accept the loss of a deduction by not providing requested information that might point the auditor to other trouble areas on your return.

• ***IRS auditors have limited resources and are under pressure to close cases.*** They are very unlikely to try to force you to produce information, even when they have the legal right to do so, if it will slow down the processing of your case without leading to any real payoff for them.

This means that you can negotiate most IRS information requests. And you don't have to fear retaliation from the IRS—such as its expanding the audit—if you try to contain the IRS's information requests.

KEY: Expanding an audit means slowing it down. This is counterproductive to the auditor—so he/she is unlikely to do it out of spite.

The only time an auditor will expand an audit is if he has a specific idea of how it will lead the IRS to a bigger tax assessment—and if he already has that idea, it is even more important that you not provide the information requested.

CONTAINING AN AUDIT...

IRS auditors have no right to fish through your tax records, but many of them will try to do so nonetheless.

IRS audit notices typically ask the taxpayer to bring to an audit the tax returns filed for the years *before* and *after* the year being examined.

But the IRS's own rules say auditors are supposed to ask only for information relevant to the specific tax year or tax issue under examination.

STRATEGY: In my practice, I ordinarily do not provide other years' returns to the IRS. If a specific item, such as a depreciation schedule, relates to more than one year, I will provide the relevant *part* of another year's return, not the whole return.

Declining to provide the extra years' tax returns has *never once* resulted in the IRS retaliating by opening another year for examination.

And while auditors can get copies of the other years' tax returns from IRS record storage facilities, this is so slow a process they rarely do.

RESULT: The auditor never sees the other years' returns, and fishing expeditions through them are averted.

More ways to contain the IRS...

• ***Have an auditor place all requests for information in writing.*** This tends to deter him from making an overbroad, burdensome or repetitious request. And if you do receive such a request, you can appeal it to the auditor's supervisor.

ALSO: Written requests avert misunderstandings that can lead to needless conflict with the auditor, and provide a record that may prove valuable if you appeal the audit's results.

• ***Have a professional represent you at an audit instead of attending yourself.*** This is a right you have under the *Taxpayer Bill of Rights.*

BENEFITS: You can't inadvertently volunteer information if you aren't there. Your professional representative will know how to minimize the auditor's requests. Because information requests must be relayed to you through your representative, these requests will slow down the audit—and this, in turn, will deter the auditor from making "speculative" requests.

• ***Never bring full records to an audit for the auditor to thumb through.*** Only bring specific records that the auditor has requested. If the auditor then wants to look at other records, have him make another written request.

SPECIAL CASES...

Even when an auditor puts a request for records in writing, as a practical matter, you do not have to comply if you are willing to have the related deduction disallowed.

The only time you are *legally required* to produce records is if the IRS serves you with a summons for them—that is, a court order requiring you to produce them.

In reality, however, the IRS *rarely* issues summonses in audits of individuals—and when it does, it rarely goes to court to enforce them even when taxpayers don't comply.

Again, the reason is that the IRS is short of resources—IRS attorneys don't want to deal with audit summonses unless there is very good reason for doing so.

RESULT: Even if you receive a summons, you usually can negotiate with the IRS to reduce its scope by complaining that it is overbroad, burdensome or repetitive. And by producing summoned records piecemeal over time, you may deter the IRS from ever acting to enforce it.

SPECIAL LEGAL DEFENSES: The following defenses can defeat any IRS information request or summons...

• ***The right against self-incrimination*** applies if records sought by the IRS include information that could be incriminating. Because a criminal matter must be involved, you should speak with an attorney before making this claim.

• ***Attorney-client privilege*** protects tax-related papers produced by a lawyer in anticipation of litigation.

EXAMPLE: If you believe that a planned tax transaction is likely to put you in court against the IRS, your lawyer's work on it will be privileged.

The privilege does not apply to just any paper prepared by a lawyer —you can't get privilege for your tax return simply by having a lawyer prepare it. Privileged documents must relate to actual or anticipated litigation.

STRATEGY: Accountant–client privilege is limited to communications in civil tax matters. For broader protection, hire a lawyer to work for you and let the lawyer hire an accountant. In this way, the accountant's work will be privileged to the extent that the lawyer's work is.

PROTECTING ASSETS...

You may also wish to keep the IRS from knowing about your assets and their value, in case you get into future tax trouble.

You can achieve this goal by transferring legal ownership of assets that you own—such as real estate, investments, vehicles, a safe-deposit box, etc.—to other legal entities that are controlled by you, to family members or to close associates.

You may transfer assets to a corporation, family limited partnership, life insurance trust or other trust. Such a transfer may...

• ***Legally insulate the assets from the IRS,*** if the other entity is not legally responsible for your taxes.

• ***Construct an information barrier*** that prevents the IRS from learning the assets exist. If they aren't held in your name, the IRS may not find them when it conducts a search to identify all the assets that are in your name.

IMPORTANT: Such transfers are perfectly legal if made before a problem with the IRS arises—even if you anticipate that a problem with the IRS might arise.

HELPFUL: Have such a transfer also serve a nontax-related purpose—perhaps related to estate planning or managing investments.

CAUTION: If you make such a transfer after a problem with the IRS arises, the courts may set it aside as a fraudulent transfer.

■

TRAPS IN LENDING MONEY TO FAMILY

Source: **David S. Rhine, CPA,** partner and national director of family wealth planning, BDO Seidman, LLP, 330 Madison Ave., New York 10017.

If you lend money to a child who proves unable to repay you, you may not be able to claim a bad debt deduction for the full amount of your loss—because...

• ***The IRS is likely to treat an intra-family transfer as a gift*** rather than a loan, and allow no deduction at all.

• ***Even when the IRS accepts that a transfer is a loan, a full deduction is allowed only for business bad debts.*** The loan to your child will be deemed a personal bad debt that produces a short-term capital loss.

Such a loss must be used to offset capital gains, with no more than $3,000 of net losses deductible against ordinary income each year, and undeducted amounts carried forward. To protect deductions...

Prove a transfer is a loan. Document it with a note, set a market rate of interest, have a repayment schedule, specify collateral, detail in writing the purpose of the loan and make efforts to collect it.

NOTE: You can't escape interest income. If you don't charge interest as required, you'll have to report imputed interest income.

■

VALUABLE WAYS TO CUT TAXES ON YOUR HOME UNDER THE NEW TAX LAW

Source: **Mark T. Watson, CPA, CFP**, partner, personal financial planning practice, KPMG Peat Marwick LLP, 200 Crescent Ct., Ste. 300, Dallas 75201.

The new tax law does much more for home owners than simply letting them take a $250,000/$500,000 tax-free gain on sale. Here are seven additional ways the law helps home owners save taxes...

• ***Meaning of "principal residence" broadened.*** A home now qualifies as a principal residence, on which you can take tax-free gain, if you've lived in and owned it for only two out of the previous five years.

So, if you moved out of your home up to three years previously, and perhaps have rented it out for profit in the meantime, it will still qualify as a residence on which you can take tax-free gain.

CONTRAST: The old law required that a home *remain your actual residence* for you to be eligible to make a tax-deferred rollover of gain into a replacement home. And if you rented your home out for profit, it would lose its "residence" status.

PLANNING: If you can't get the price you want for a home that you've lived in and owned for two years, you can rent it out for up to three years, while waiting for prices to rise, before you sell—and still take tax-free gain on the sale.

• ***You can take tax-free gain multiple times.*** Old law allowed an up-to-$125,000 exclusion of gain on a home sale for persons age 55 and older, but only once in a lifetime.

The new law allows you to use the $250,000/$500,000 exclusion once every two years regardless of your age.

EXAMPLE: In addition to your regular home, you own a vacation home and also a rental property that you lease out for profit. All three have risen greatly in value since you bought them.

If you change your principal residence from your current home to the vacation home and then to the rental property, and live at least two years in each, you may be able to claim the $250,000/$500,000 exclusion for all three.

• ***You can use both the new-law and old-law exclusions.*** You can use the new law's $250,000/ $500,000 tax exclusion even if you've already used the once-in-a-lifetime exclusion of the old law.

OPPORTUNITY: You can still use the old law's exclusion on a home sale that occurred within the last three years—and perhaps obtain a tax *refund* by doing so.

KEY: Under old law, persons at least age 55 who sold a home for a gain of only a few thousand dollars might have chosen not to use the once-in-a-lifetime exclusion, and elected instead to "save" it in case they realized a larger gain on another home sale later.

Those who saved the old law's exclusion in this manner and who paid tax as a result, can claim the old law's exclusion now. File an amended tax return, IRS Form 1040X, for the year in which the sale took place and claim a refund (as long as the statute of limitations has not expired for the year of the sale).

• ***New rules for home offices.*** The new law *appears to be* more favorable (that is, until the IRS or courts provide guidance) regarding home offices. **HOW...**

• If there was no home office use in at least two of the five years preceding the sale, then the exclusion applies to the entire home (no allocation is required for the home office).

EXAMPLE: Sue owned and used her entire home as her principal residence from May 1994 to May 1996 (two full years). In 1997, Sue began using a portion of her house as a home office. If Sue sells her home in 1998, she does not have to apportion the gain and can use the exclusion for all of the gain. She owned and used the entire home for personal use for at least two out of five years before the date of sale.

DEPRECIATION DEDUCTIONS: Those taken for the home office on or before May 6, 1997, are not recaptured and taxed. This depreciation reduces the seller's basis in the home, and so therefore increases gain on the sale. That gain qualifies for the $250,000/$500,000 exclusion.

• In 1999, a home-office deduction will be available for persons who manage or administer a business from home even if they primarily work elsewhere. *Key:* They must have no other place to do managerial and administration tasks.

Current law generally allows a home-office deduction only if the office is your principal place of business. This bars the deduction in 1998 to many people who genuinely use a home office for recordkeeping and management tasks, but who perform work tasks elsewhere.

BONUS: With the establishment of a deductible home office, nondeductible commuting expenses can become deductible business travel.

It may also make it easier to expense the cost of a computer. Commuting from home to work is not deductible, but travel between two work sites is deductible—and a home office qualifies a home as a work site.

• ***Transfers of homes to children made easier.*** Some parents who approach retirement age desire to make a gift of the family residence to their grown children.

Until now, the drawback to this was that when a home had appreciated in value, for income tax purposes it was better for children to receive it by inheritance than by gift.

REASON: Inherited property receives a "stepped-up basis" —the heir's basis in the property is set at the property's current market value. So a child who receives a home by inheritance avoids all taxable gain on the home's appreciation in value to date.

CONTRAST: The recipient of a gift generally obtains the same basis in the gift property that the donor had. So a child who received an appreciated home by gift could face a large taxable gain on its future sale.

OPPORTUNITY: The new tax law eliminates this problem for many by enabling a child who receives a home by gift to use the $250,000/ $500,000 exclusion to eliminate the gains tax that otherwise would be due, provided the child uses the home as his/her principal residence for at least two years.

• ***Residence status in marital separations protected.*** The new law preserves the $250,000/$500,000 exclusion for spouses who are required to move out of a home under the terms of a separation agreement.

If a divorce or separation instrument requires you to leave your home while your spouse continues to reside in it, you can count the period of your spouse's use as your own "residential use" of the home when determining whether you are eligible to claim the exclusion. Even though you don't live in the house you will be treated as if you do.

This could save the exclusion for those who actually live in a house for less than two years due to such a court order or in situations where the house is sold many years later, after the children are grown.

• ***Gain may be tax free even if you sell early.*** Even if you fail to live in a home for the required two years, you may still be able to exclude some or all of your gain on its sale from your income.

RULE: If you move from your home before the two years are up due to a change in your place of employment, for medical reasons or due to other "unforeseen circumstances," a reduced exclusion remains available to you.

In such a case, the amount of gain you may exclude from income is a fraction of the $250,000/$500,000 amount that equals the fraction represented by the amount of time you resided in the home in two years.

EXAMPLE: If you resided in the home for 18 months, your permitted exclusion equals 75% of the $250,000/$500,000 tax-free amount—this equals $187,500 on a single return or $375,000 on a joint return.

In practice, this means your whole gain probably will be tax free, since it is unlikely a house will appreciate in value by a greater amount in such a short period of time.

■

$637,000 GIFT FROM THE IRS

Leroy Stanley settled a complex tax dispute with the IRS by making a payment to it.

But the IRS miscredited the payment and sent him a $637,000 refund by mistake. It didn't realize the mistake until more than two years had passed, after which it demanded return of the refund.

COURT: For Stanley. To recover the refund the IRS either had to reassess the tax before the statute of limitations expired, or sue for the return of the refund within two years. It had missed both deadlines—so Stanley was allowed to keep the money.

Leroy P. Stanley, Fed. Cir., 98-1 USTC ¶50,304.

■

TAXPAYER VICTORIES THAT CAN HELP EACH OF US ONE WAY OR ANOTHER

Over the past year, many taxpayers were victorious in cases against the IRS. Their triumphs may help you plan ways to save taxes...

• ***Expenses are deductible without records.*** The Tax Court let the owner of a small business deduct expenses without records after he showed that his records had been destroyed in a fire.

RATIONALE: The business was legitimate so it *must* have had expenses, and the owner's testimony about them was credible.

The Court allowed all the claimed deductions except those for which the Tax Code requires specific documentation—driving costs and business meals.

Eugene C. Joseph, Sr., TC Memo 1997-447.

• ***IRS can't demand records it lost.*** The IRS said Michael McKenzie had filed no tax returns for four years and tried to collect back taxes for those years. But McKenzie said he had indeed filed the returns and that the IRS had lost his copies after seizing his records in an earlier dispute.

JUDGE: "No court could justifiably allow a party to have destroyed the only evidence that the other party may have in its defense, and then claim to win because the other party has not met his burden." The missing returns will be deemed filed.

Michael J. McKenzie, Bankr. N.D. Ohio, No. 97-3161.

• ***Taxpayer keeps $93,000 mistaken refund.*** Carroll Singleton requested a $30,000 tax refund, but the IRS said a $123,000 refund was due and sent it. Later, the IRS demanded $93,000 back, but Singleton said the IRS hadn't filed a notice assessing the $93,000 before the deadline for doing so expired, so he could keep the money. The IRS replied that it doesn't have to send such a notice to recover a *nonrebate refund*—one that results from an error made when tallying up the numbers on a return.

COURT OF APPEALS: The matter was considered a rebate because the IRS had recalculated the tax due when making its mistake. Moreover, the courts have consistently rejected the IRS's distinction between *rebate* and *nonrebate* refunds. Singleton was allowed to keep the money.

Carroll Eugene Singleton, CA-4, No. 96-1924.

• ***Interest paid on divorce property settlement is deductible.*** Under the terms of a divorce, the wife transferred her interests in several valuable assets to the husband, who in return agreed to pay her $600,000 over ten years at 10% interest. The husband then deducted the interest he paid on the note. But the IRS objected that interest payments made as part of an asset division are a nondeductible personal expense.

TAX COURT: Interest is deductible if it is allocated to items that produce deductible interest expenses under normal tax rules—such as a residence, and business and investment properties.

John L. Seymour, 109 TC No. 14.

• ***IRS must release its own expert's valuation of donated property.*** Richard Bennett claimed a $236,000 deduction for items that he donated to charity. But the IRS disallowed the deduction, saying the items had *no* value.

Bennett then learned that the IRS had attained two appraisals of the donated items—and that after the first appraisal found the items were valuable, the IRS had obtained a second opinion from another appraiser who said they had no value. The IRS then acted solely on the basis of the second appraisal. Bennett demanded that the IRS release its initial appraisal to him. But the IRS refused, arguing that because it hadn't used the initial appraisal, it was irrelevant to the case.

COURT: The appraisal was relevant to the issue of the items' value, so the IRS must produce it.

Richard L. Bennett, TC Memo 1997-505.

• ***Smart couple beats the IRS.*** When a couple saw that they faced a big tax bill, the husband declared bankruptcy but his wife did not. The IRS then assessed a $300,000 tax liability on their joint returns and said it would go after the wife's assets.

COURT: Going after the wife's assets would reduce the husband's ability to complete his financial reorganization plan. The wife had intended to pay the couple's household expenses—freeing the husband to pay his creditors. But if the IRS took her assets, this would be impossible and the plan would fail. So the IRS levy on her assets was ordered *lifted.*

In re: **Gregory B. Miller,** Bankr. S.D. Ala., No. 97-11671.

• ***Beat the IRS to the courthouse to get paid first.*** Patricia Read's former husband fell behind on the alimony he owed her and the taxes he owed the IRS.

She obtained a judgment against him and filed a seizure notice against a trust that held his funds. Then the IRS filed a lien on the same trust—but there wasn't enough money to pay both of them.

COURT: Patricia Read filed her judgment *first,* so she gets paid first.

Read v. US, E.D. La., No. 95-4036.

• ***IRS pays penalty for ignoring taxpayer for years.*** The estate of Paul Rao spent *four years* trying to inform the IRS that a gift tax assessment the IRS had sent was in error. Then the IRS put a lien on the estate's property.

The estate responded by filing a case in court, at which point the IRS's lawyers quickly conceded—before the court heard the case.

The estate then asked the court to order the IRS to pay the legal fees it had incurred. The IRS objected that the court had no jurisdiction to do so because it hadn't decided the case.

RULING: The court's acceptance of the case is what caused the IRS to concede. So the court has jurisdiction—and the IRS has to pay.

Estate of Paul P. Rao, S.D. N.Y., No. 97 Civ. 3455.

• ***Wrong street number voids tax-deficiency notice.*** The IRS mailed a deficiency notice to street address number "750" instead of "705." The IRS said this mix-up didn't matter because the local mail carrier knew the addressee and tried to deliver the notice to the correct address. However, the mail carrier did not testify.

TAX COURT: The deficiency notice had been mailed to the wrong address and the IRS had no evidence showing the envelope had actually been delivered to the right address—so the notice was invalid.

Keith Lee Wilson, TC Memo 1997-515.

■

FOOLISH MISTAKES PEOPLE MAKE WHEN PREPARING THEIR RETURNS

Source: **Ms. X, Esq.,** a former IRS agent who is still well connected.

You'd be surprised at how many taxpayers cut their income tax liability by claiming deductions that are clearly false.

COMMON TAX LIES: Taking dependency exemptions for children who no longer qualify as dependents, or children who never existed, or relatives the taxpayer only minimally supports.

OTHER ILLEGAL TRICKS: Reducing capital gains by inflating the cost basis of stocks sold...and completely fabricating unreimbursed employee business expense deductions for auto expenses and entertainment costs.

■

5
SURVIVING AN AUDIT

CHECKLIST: HOW TO AUDIT-PROOF YOUR TAX RETURN

Source: **Craig A. Minnick, CPA, JD,** managing director of American Express Tax & Business Services Inc., One S. Wacker Dr., Suite 1700, Chicago 60606.

The last thing you want to do is stick red flags on your tax return inviting the IRS to look over the numbers. Be careful. Do all you can to make your return audit-proof.

BASICS...

• ***ID numbers.*** Be sure you have the right Social Security numbers for you and your dependents (regardless of age). If you're adopting a child, you can get a temporary tax ID number by filing IRS Form W-7A (Form W-7 if it's a foreign adoption).

• ***Filing status.*** Make sure you've used the most advantageous filing status. Marital status is determined as of December 31, so if you're married on that date, you can file a joint return. If you're separated and have dependents, see whether you qualify for head-of-household status.

• ***Dependency exemptions.*** If you're claiming an exemption under a multiple support agreement, or for your child who lives with his/her other parent, make sure you file a signed Form 2120 for a multiple support agreement or Form 8332 for waiver of the exemption for the child by the custodial parent.

GROSS INCOME...

• ***Matching.*** Make sure that the figures for salary, interest, dividends, pensions and annuities you report match the numbers on information returns you received (Form W-2 for wages and a type of Form 1099 for most other income).

If you're reporting a different amount, it's advisable to put the W-2 or 1099 amount on your return, show how you adjusted it to come up with the right figure, and attach an explanation. *Reason:* IRS computers match returns against W-2s and 1099s and will pick up any discrepancies.

• ***Loss traps.*** Don't deduct losses you are not entitled to take, including...

• Losses on mutual fund shares where you've reinvested dividends within 30 days of the sale. This violates the wash-sale rules and makes any loss nondeductible.

• Losses on personal assets—such as your home or a car—not used for business.

• Losses from passive activities in excess of passive activity income.

• Unused capital losses of a spouse who died in a prior year.

ADJUSTMENTS TO GROSS INCOME...

• ***IRA traps.*** Don't claim the following IRA transactions as deductions on your 1998 return...

•Contributions made after April 15, 1999, even if you obtain a filing extension.

•Rollovers.

•Contributions made between January 1, 1998, and April 15, 1998, that you deducted on your 1997 return.

• ***Divorce.*** Child support and voluntary alimony payments aren't deductible. Be sure to include the Social Security number of the person to whom you pay alimony (the IRS matches your deduction with the income reported on the recipient's return).

• ***Relocating retirees.*** Don't deduct moving expenses if you have retired and are relocating.

DEDUCTIONS AND TAX COMPUTATION...

• ***Extra deduction.*** If you're 65 or older and/or blind, claim the additional standard deduction amount if you don't itemize deductions.

• ***Charity.*** Make sure you received written acknowledgments from any charity to which you made a contribution of $250 or more (a canceled check isn't good enough).

• ***State estimated payments.*** Don't deduct your fourth-quarter 1998 state and local taxes paid in 1999 (they will be deductible on your 1999 return).

• ***Reimbursement trap.*** Don't deduct your commuting costs or any employee expenses for which you were reimbursed under your employer's accountable plan.

• ***Gamblers' trap.*** Unless you're a professional gambler, don't deduct gambling losses in excess of your winnings (and make sure you can prove your losses with a diary, ticket stubs, etc.).

• ***Employee business expenses.*** Don't try to claim miscellaneous deductions on a Schedule C if they're *employee* business expenses. These expenses are only deductible as itemized deductions on Schedule A.

• ***Find the right column.*** If you use the tax tables to figure your tax, be sure to look under the correct column for your filing status. (Using the wrong column is one of the most common errors that taxpayers make.) If you have any long-term capital gains, use Schedule D to figure your tax.

TAX CREDITS...

• ***Child care.*** If you've received child-care or adoption benefits from your employer, don't claim a credit for the same expenses. But if you're entitled to claim a child-care credit for your out-of-pocket expenses, don't forget to include the tax ID number of the child-care provider.

• ***Social Security tax overpayments.*** If you worked for more than one employer in 1998 and earned more than $68,400, don't forget to take a credit for any excess Social Security taxes you paid.

OTHER TAXES...

• ***Self-employment.*** Be sure to figure self-employment tax if you had self-employment income of at least $400.

• ***Early withdrawals.*** If you took a distribution from a qualified retirement plan, IRA or commercial annuity before you turned

59½, be sure to include a 10% early distribution penalty unless an exception applies.

• ***Alternative Minimum Tax (AMT).*** Check whether you're liable for any AMT, especially if you exercised incentive stock options or held private activity bonds.

• ***Nanny tax.*** If you had a household employee in 1998 and you paid at least $1,100 in wages, be sure to figure employment taxes and include payment with your return.

FINAL CHECK OF YOUR RETURN...

• ***Form and date.*** Make sure your payment check includes your Social Security number and the year and return number (e.g., "1998 Form 1040").

• ***1099s and W-2s.*** Attach all W-2s and the 1099s that show any taxes you paid. Don't attach other 1099s or Schedule K-1s.

• ***Check and recheck.*** Math mistakes are common. *Problem:* They can easily lead to IRS questions.

• ***Sign and date.*** Make sure you (and your spouse) sign and date your return.

• ***Mailing/filing.*** Use the correct postage (if the return is more than five pages, a 33¢ stamp is not enough). *Better still:* File using registered or certified mail as proof that the return was filed on time. Alternatively, use an IRS-approved private carrier such as Federal Express.

■

HOW TO FIGHT A NIGHTMARE AUDIT WITH THE IRS...AND WIN!

Source: **Edgar H. Gee, Jr., CPA,** and **Willis Jackson, Esq.,** 602 S. Gay St., Ste. 702, Knoxville, TN 37902. Mr. Gee's testimony before Congress led to favorable new law regarding independent contractors. He is coauthor of *Guide to Worker Classification Issues.* Practitioners Publishing Co. Willis Jackson has successfully tried numerous independent contractor cases.

We have seen real-life nightmares of IRS auditors simply ignoring the Internal Revenue Code, court decisions and the IRS's own rules to impose huge tax bills on our clients.

The methods we use to overwhelm the most intransigent of auditors can work for you, too.

PLAN YOUR PLAN...

It's time to adopt a new attitude toward the IRS when you find it ignoring the law and its own rules to hit you with a big, unjustified tax bill. The IRS's behavior puts you in an adversarial relationship.

In routine dealings with the IRS, you and your tax advisers probably defer to IRS requests for paperwork and information.

But when the IRS ignores the law or its own rules, you have to be willing to say *no* and take the offensive. This is a big switch in approach, but you must make it. Here's how...

• ***Don't talk to the IRS yourself.*** Whenever you, the taxpayer, speak to an IRS auditor, you give the IRS a big advantage...

• The auditor can ask you any questions he/she wants, which may send the audit off in a new direction. So you give the IRS the initiative.

• It's only human nature to be intimidated by an auditor, so you give the IRS a big psychological advantage, too.

The Taxpayer Bill of Rights says you don't have to meet with an IRS auditor personally. Use that right. Have the auditor communicate through your representative.

STAND UP TO THE IRS...

You don't have to comply with every request the auditor makes.

EXAMPLE: It's a common IRS tactic to bury the taxpayer with requests for records and proof. These requests often are an attempt by the IRS to get the taxpayer to do its work.

KEY: The IRS often is thought of as omniscient—but this is not so. For instance, the IRS's computer system is an utter travesty. Also, most auditors have little knowledge of the details of how real businesses operate.

REALITY: The IRS auditor very likely knows much *less* than you fear. But if you accede to every IRS request for information, you may give the auditor rewarding opportunities to look for trouble.

DEFENSE: The Tax Code and the IRS's own rules say you do not have to comply with IRS information requests that you reasonably determine to be irrelevant, immaterial or undiscoverable because they relate to a year closed under the statute of limitations.

Of course, the auditor won't tell you that you don't have to comply with his requests—and probably will insist that you *do* comply.

REQUIRED: A litigator who knows which IRS requests you do and do not have to respond to, and how to frame responses that give the IRS exactly the information to which it is entitled and no more.

• ***Have a solid strategy.*** Meet with your adviser and form a strategy for handling your case all the way through—from dealing with the auditor to going to court. **KEYS...**

• Truly know the strengths and weaknesses of your case.

• Anticipate the IRS's responses and prepare your counter-responses.

• At each level, prepare the groundwork for success at the next level. Let the IRS agent know you are prepared to go over his head to the next level.

• If there is disagreement on your side about the approach to take against the IRS, resolve it in advance. You don't want disputes to arise on your side of the table during a meeting with the IRS.

• As a client, know the result you wish to obtain and the steps you are willing to take to get it—including the amount of fees you are willing to pay your advisers.

TRAP: If you balk and change your mind halfway through the case, the result will be costly for you.

• ***Prepare, prepare.*** Your first chance to end a nightmare audit—and best chance to end it at relatively low cost—is at a meeting with the auditor's supervisor.

For this meeting you should know the tax law and the IRS's own rules better than the IRS does. This is not as hard as it sounds. One of the IRS's biggest problems is retaining capable personnel. The IRS auditor you deal with very likely will be less educated, less experienced and lower paid than your own expert adviser. **IN ADDITION...**

• IRS agents divide their time among many cases.

• They generally work only 9 am to 5 pm and take lots of vacation time.

• They are slow to be trained on new court rulings, changes in the Tax Code and IRS rules.

You, on the other hand, have the opportunity and motivation to obtain deep knowledge of the latest developments in the law and in IRS policy affecting you.

EXAMPLE: In our recent independent contractor audit, neither the IRS auditor nor his supervisor had received new IRS training on...

• The changes in the law enacted by the *Small Business Job Protection Act of 1996.*

• New procedures adopted by the IRS regarding independent contractors.

The result was that at our meeting with the auditor's supervisor we were able to present *the IRS's own auditor training materials* that flatly contradicted the position they had taken until then. The members of the IRS team at the meeting soon were contradicting each other and arguing among themselves.

TAKE THE OFFENSIVE...

If you are caught up in a nightmare audit, then by definition the auditor has ignored either the law or IRS procedures.

AIM: To make this as clear as possible and take the offensive against IRS personnel who have flouted the rules they are supposed to follow.

The IRS isn't good on the defensive—IRS auditors aren't used to defending themselves and usually aren't very good at it.

When you point out that the auditor has ignored the law, court decisions or IRS rules, expect these standard responses...

• ***Denial.*** The auditor simply says it's not so.

RESPONSE: Repeat your position and demand that the auditor address it in writing in the audit report, so it can be reviewed on appeal.

• ***Distraction.*** The auditor may raise a host of new problems, and issue new document requests.

RESPONSE: Don't be distracted. Continue to insist that the auditor address your defenses in writing in the audit report.

Show that you are quite prepared to quickly take the matter the next step up—to the auditor's supervisor, to IRS Appeals or to court. New developments give you real leverage when you show you are willing to fight an auditor's unjustified position...

• The *Taxpayer Relief Act of 1997* makes the IRS pay litigation costs when the IRS violates its own procedures in a tax dispute—and gives IRS management new power to discipline personally individual agents who are responsible for such abuses.

• As a result of highly publicized Congressional hearings into IRS abuses, IRS management is getting tougher on abusive agents in order to protect the agency.

The IRS commissioner dismissed a great many agents for acts of abuse. Therefore, abusive agents *do* have something to fear, i.e., being fired.

RESULT: If you make a strong case to an agent or the agent's manager that an audit finding violates the law or the IRS's own rules, they now have good reason to think twice before letting you bring the matter to their superiors.

ECONOMICAL ADVICE...

Expert advice is vital for litigating a dispute with the IRS—but it is also expensive.

STRATEGY: If not enough tax dollars are at stake to hire a tax litigation expert, have your regular tax adviser consult with one.

You'll be able to obtain the basics of your litigation strategy at a fraction of the cost.

■

HOW TO GET YOUR WAY WITH AN IRS AUDITOR

Source: **Ed Slott, CPA,** E. Slott & Co., CPAs, 100 Merrick Rd., Rockville Centre, NY 11570. He is editor and publisher of *Ed Slott's IRA Advisor* and author of *Your Tax Questions Answered, 1998 Edition.* Plymouth Press.

There's no need to go to war with an IRS auditor. In fact, by making friends with the auditor, you're likely to get a much better audit result.

It may be hard to imagine that you can get an IRS auditor to work with you instead of against you on a tax problem, and that you may even be friendly with each other. But it is possible. And it can have a big payoff on your final tax bill.

KEY: IRS auditors are given tremendous discretion. It's up to the auditor to...

- Allow or disallow items on your tax return, based on the auditor's own personal opinions.
- Impose or not impose penalties on your return.
- Write up an audit report that describes your case in sympathetic or hostile terms. *Key:* This report will go with your case to IRS Appeals, and to court if you go that far. It's the first thing that will be reviewed by an IRS Appeals Officer or Tax Court judge, and it is important.

Remember that auditors are people—and you don't get what you want from people by making enemies of them.

OBJECTIVE...

Your goal should be to close your case at the audit level as quickly as possible—at the first meeting with the auditor if you can.

WHY: The higher you go in the appeals process, the more will be required of you in proof and formal documentation. And—the more you'll pay in professional fees and personal effort that could be spent on other matters.

Also, during the appeals process the IRS position may harden as statements are placed in writing and IRS agents feel the need to justify positions they have taken.

So it's much better to finish everything during your first meeting with the auditor.

This usually is possible with personal audits. Business audits are more likely to require more than one meeting, but the same principle applies—close the matter at the audit level if at all possible, and as quickly as you can.

HOW TO GET IT...

You get what you want from an IRS auditor the same way you'd get what you want from any other human being—by treating the auditor with dignity and respect and not provoking any needless conflict. How to go about it...

- ***Never tell an auditor, "You're wrong...I'm right."*** This is the same as saying, "You're stupid, and I'm smart"—and it's no way to win over another person to your way of seeing things.

It may be that your position is entirely correct, but if you drive the auditor into a hostile stance, you may not be able to prove it without going to IRS Appeals—with all the cost in time, money and aggravation that that involves.

TRAP: A hostile auditor may much more aggressively examine other items on your tax return.

It's much better to help the auditor realize on his own what the correct position is.

EXAMPLE: When an auditor made a blatant error concerning depreciation deductions on a return, I didn't say, "You're wrong."

Instead, I said, "I thought that was the right way to do it, and I'm afraid I may have made the same mistake on other clients' returns. Could you show me where I went wrong?"

The auditor replied, "Sure," looked in a reference book, and quickly came back with, "Hey, don't worry, you were right all along!"

RESULT: The fact that the auditor had made a mistake never came up. Instead, the auditor emerged thinking that he'd helped me! And the goodwill that resulted carried over into other parts of the audit.

• ***If you decide to go to IRS Appeals, get your viewpoint included in the auditor's report.***

Another reason to be friendly with the auditor is so that he will recognize you have a reasonable argument and include it in his audit report, even if he disagrees with it.

CRITICAL: The audit report will travel with your case as high as it goes in the appeals process, and have a big impact on those who review it.

EXAMPLE: An auditor disallowed a $100,000 item on a client's return, saying he understood our argument but didn't agree. I asked, "OK, but could you explain our position in your audit report?" and he did.

At IRS Appeals, the first thing the Appeals Officer did was read the auditor's report. He then looked up and said, "It sounds like the auditor understood your position but just couldn't bring himself to sign off on a $100,000 deduction." The Appeals Officer gave us 90% of what we'd asked for.

The result might have been different if the auditor had filed a hostile report saying we were using dubious tactics to avoid taxes.

• ***Be prepared.*** Thorough preparation is vital for an audit—the result of an audit is 90% determined by the preparation you do before you meet the auditor.

Your preparation provides you with both the substantive arguments you will make to the auditor and the psychological tactics you can use.

KEY: Auditors don't want to waste time any more than you do. They want to close cases quickly, just as taxpayers do—and you can take advantage of this.

HOW: The audit notice will detail exactly what the IRS wants to look at, probably several things.

You should pull together your records for each item in a separate clipped-together pile or in a folder, with a summary (and an adding machine tape, if appropriate).

KEY: Make each group of records look good.

Then present the records to the auditor. If your records look good and it's clear you're not hiding anything, the auditor is likely to think there's nothing to be found in them—and that he'd be wasting his time rooting through them.

He'll very likely just sample one or two groups of records, and if they are in order, that may be all that gets looked at.

Even if the auditor does go through all your records, he'll do so with a different attitude—believing you're honest and well intentioned rather than hiding anything.

This can make a big difference in the auditor's approach to any "gray area" items he comes across, and to whether or not he adds penalties to any mistakes he does find.

CONTRAST: If you present disorganized records to an auditor and challenge him to find problems in them, he will find them.

• ***Take control of the audit.*** When an audit involves several items, it has to start somewhere. Your preparation will reveal which of the items your position is strongest on, and where it is the weakest.

Take control of the audit by bringing up your strongest items first. Simply say something like, "Let's start with this, it's on top of my pile."

The auditor is supposed to look at everything anyhow, so there is no reason for him not to agree.

IMPORTANCE: Making a strong first impression builds your credibility. The auditor is likely to think that all your records are as strong as the first group he sees—so there is no point in spending a lot of time scrutinizing them.

• ***Don't bring consultants to the audit.*** There's no point in bringing in expensive, high-powered consultants and advisers to an initial audit meeting. All it will do is get the IRS thinking about what you are trying to protect.

The IRS will respond by bringing in its own experts from the start, giving your case much more scrutiny.

Send just one person to the initial audit, yourself or a single professional adviser. This keeps the pressure low on the IRS auditor, which is what you want.

It may be a good idea to consult with specialist advisers before the initial audit meeting, but keep them out of sight at the first meeting.

If that meeting goes poorly, you can always bring in the "heavy artillery" later. But the initial audit meeting will be more likely to go well if you keep the pressure on the auditor low.

• ***Ask what it will take to close the case.*** Auditors want to close cases quickly. If you ask the auditor toward the end of the audit, "What will it take to close this right now?" you'll probably get a positive response.

KEY: Before the audit meeting, decide for yourself or with your tax adviser what an acceptable "bottom line" from the auditor will be.

An auditor has to document each examination as if it were going all the way to Tax Court and is recording every argument and gray area the IRS can use against you.

But if you tell the auditor you are willing to close now, all that pressure is relieved from the auditor and he'll be much more likely to set aside the picky details and give you an answer you both can accept.

• ***Have an ace in the hole.*** Have a deduction that you and your accountants overlooked on the original return—you usually can find one. You can use it to counter whatever extra tax the auditor chooses to assess and make it part of your "close now" agreement.

KEY: Bring up the extra deduction only after the auditor tells you the final number for any tax shortfall he has determined—that way you will get full benefit from it.

If you bring up the extra deduction at the beginning of the audit, the auditor may feel he is starting out behind and give your return extra scrutiny to try to get back the tax he's lost.

■

TAX LOOPHOLES AFTER THE AUDIT YES...AFTER THE AUDIT!

Source: **Edward Mendlowitz, CPA,** partner, Mendlowitz Weitsen, LLP, CPAs, Two Pennsylvania Plaza, New York 10121. He is author of several books on taxes, including *New Tax Traps/New Opportunities.* Boardroom Special Reports.

If your tax return is audited, chances are the examining agent will assess extra tax—at least nine out of ten audits result in more tax being assessed.

Fortunately, the agent's idea of how much tax you owe is not the last word on the matter.

Even after the audit, you have many opportunities to settle your tax bill on more favorable terms. Some, if not all, of the extra tax can be wiped away by appealing the agent's conclusions. *How to appeal...*

THE SUPERVISOR...

When the audit is concluded, the agent will take some time to write up a "revenue agent's report."

LOOPHOLE: Before this report is written, tell the agent you'd like to have a meeting with his/her supervisor.

Like most rank-and-file employees, IRS agents don't want to annoy their immediate bosses. Some agents may be willing to reduce a tax assessment just to avoid such a meeting.

STRATEGY: Don't threaten or antagonize the examining agent, but subtly suggest that you will take matters up with his supervisor if that is necessary.

LOOPHOLE: Actually meet with the supervisor. If the agent doesn't budge, you are well within your rights to present your case to the supervisor. At this level, there may be more willingness to offer you a deal, in order to close your file.

Unlike agents, supervisors can "trade issues," giving you the benefit of the doubt in an area where your case is strong in return for your concession elsewhere.

30-DAY LETTER...

When you don't get anywhere with either the agent or the supervisor, you'll eventually receive a formal notice from the IRS called a "30-day letter."

This means you have 30 days from the *date the letter was mailed*—not the date you received it—to appeal the agent's report to the IRS's Appeals Office. This is usually done by writing a "protest letter."

LOOPHOLE: If you can't file your protest in time, you can request an extension for another 30 to 60 days. If the extension is granted by phone, be sure to send the IRS a confirmation letter immediately.

QUICK WAY TO APPEAL: If the amount in question is no more than $2,500, you can skip writing a formal appeal request and make an appointment for an appeal with a phone call.

Should you appeal? Definitely. An appeal gives you another chance to find a sympathetic IRS official who'll offer you desirable terms.

STRATEGY: The higher up the IRS ladder you go, the greater the person's authority to reach a settlement. According to IRS statistics, about 85% of the cases brought as far as IRS appeals officers are settled at that level.

LIMITATION PERIOD: At some point in the negotiations the IRS will ask you to waive the three-year statute of limitations on assessing tax deficiencies. You'll be threatened with a much bigger tax assessment, right away, if you don't grant the IRS an extension.

WHEN TO AGREE: When there still are many issues to discuss with the IRS. Without an extension, you won't have a chance to argue your points.

WHEN TO DISAGREE: If you're already facing a huge assessment, consult with a tax pro about refusing to sign a waiver of the limitation period. You may not have much to lose, and forcing the pace may lead the IRS into making assessments that they can't support. If you can show that some of the assessments the IRS made were incorrect, you'll be in a stronger position in subsequent negotiations.

90-DAY LETTER...

After your appeal, assuming it was unsuccessful, the IRS will send you a Notice of Deficiency—also known as a "90-day letter."

NOTE: You'll also get this notice if you ignore your 30-day letter. The deficiency notice will spell out exactly how much tax the IRS wants from you.

LOOPHOLE: As soon as you receive the 90-day letter, send the IRS an amount slightly less than the amount assessed. Notify them that you're making a "cash deposit in the nature of a cash bond." This will stop the interest from running while your case is still pending. You can get all or some of your deposit back if you prevail or reach a settlement.

TRAP: If you don't make this deposit, interest will compound. The interest rate on tax deficiencies (currently 9%) is higher than the interest rate you can earn on low-risk, short-term investments.

STRATEGY: Don't pay the full amount of the assessment. This will retain all your rights of disagreement, including going to Tax Court.

EXAMPLE: If you're assessed $40,000, then send $35,000. If you send $40,000, the IRS might consider the amount paid up and your case closed. You won't be able to sue in Tax Court.

LOOPHOLE: The IRS has instituted problem-solving days at its offices. On these days, any problem can be dealt with on a walk-in basis including unagreed audits of tax returns. The IRS is very anxious for this program to work and is bending over backward to accommodate taxpayers with problems. *Best:* Make a prior appointment so that the agents on staff can familiarize themselves with your situation.

TICKET TO TAX COURT...

Once you've received your 90-day letter, you can file a petition to present your case in Tax Court.

LOOPHOLE: If less than $50,000 is involved, you can litigate in "small claims" Tax Court. It is less formal and less expensive than having your case heard in regular Tax Court. You don't need to hire an attorney to litigate under the small tax cases rules.

TRAP: No appeals are permitted on decisions made in small tax cases.

STRATEGY: After you've filed your Tax Court petition, pay the balance of the amount assessed—the last $5,000 in the above example. This will keep you from having to pay any more interest if you lose.

CHOICE OF COURTS: You don't have to go to Tax Court. You can pay the tax and sue for a refund in the US Court of Federal Claims or a US District Court.

LOOPHOLE: Research may show that one of these courts has decided a similar case in your favor. Or, you may find that although the Tax Court has decided a similar case against you, these courts have not yet given an opinion on the issue. Advantages of going to Tax Court...

- ***The judges are tax specialists.*** If the law is on your side, you likely will have the best chance there.
- ***You'll have yet another conference with the IRS*** before your case is on the docket, in order to agree upon the facts. Here, the IRS representative is permitted to consider the "hazards of litigation" while negotiating, i.e., the odds of the IRS losing in court and the case setting a precedent the IRS doesn't want because it will apply favorably to other taxpayers.

EXAMPLE: Your assessment is $40,000. The IRS representative decides, based on past Tax Court decisions, that you have a 30% chance of winning in court. You might be offered a settlement at 30% below the full amount—$28,000 in this case.

At this stage, IRS officials can do virtually anything they feel is reasonable to settle a case. They'll cut deals in order to keep the Tax Court docket down to cases they think are slam-dunk IRS victories. The IRS hates losing cases that set pro-taxpayer precedents.

In practice, a very small percentage of the petitions filed for Tax Court wind up being heard by the court. If you don't get any kind of a settlement offer, you likely are going to suffer a total defeat in court, so you might want to concede and cut your losses.

Don't give up. As you go through your post-audit options, keep in mind that most sections of the Internal Revenue Code are open to interpretation. As long as you have some reasonable basis for the positions you've taken, and adequate documentation, keep fighting until you obtain a favorable settlement.

Many, many cases are settled on surprisingly attractive terms...for the taxpayer.

■